MONGOOSES DART, COBRAS STRIKE

HUNTER AND HUNTED
ANIMAL SURVIVAL

GABRIEL MERRICK

PowerKiDS press.

New York

Published in 2018 by The Rosen Publishing Group, Inc.
29 East 21st Street, New York, NY 10010

Copyright © 2018 by The Rosen Publishing Group, Inc.

All rights reserved. No part of this book may be reproduced in any form without permission in writing from the publisher, except by a reviewer.

First Edition

Editor: Theresa Morlock
Book Design: Reann Nye

Photo Credits: Cover (mongoose), pp. 6, 11 Utopia_88/Shutterstock.com; cover (cobra), pp. 1, 13 Skynavin/Shutterstock.com; p. 4 AlinaMD/Shutterstock.com; p. 5 Cvijun/Shutterstock.com; p. 7 (dwarf mongoose) feathercollector/Shutterstock.com; p. 7 (banded mongoose) Dennis Jacobsen/Shutterstock.com; p. 7 (Indian gray mongoose) CRS PHOTO/Shutterstock.com; p. 8 swapan banik/Shutterstock.com; p. 9 Martin Pelanek/Shutterstock.com; p. 10 P.V.R.M/Shutterstock.com; pp. 12, 14 Aleksandar Kamasi/Shutterstock.com; pp. 15, 16 Malcolm Schuyl/Corbis Documentary/Getty Images; p. 17 (top) GraphicsRF/Shutterstock.com; p. 17 (bottom) hangingpixels/Shutterstock.com; p. 18 Nishant Shah/Moment/Getty Images; p. 19 © oariff/iStockphoto.com; p. 20 Dezay/Shutterstock.com; p. 21 Belinda Wright/Oxford Scientific/Getty Images; p. 22 (mongoose) Manu M Nair/Shutterstock.com; p. 22 (cobra) KentaStudio/Shutterstock.com.

Cataloging-in-Publication Data

Names: Merrick, Gabriel.
Title: Mongooses dart, cobras strike / Gabriel Merrick.
Description: New York : PowerKids Press, 2018. | Series: Hunter and hunted: animal survival | Includes index.
Identifiers: ISBN 9781508156703 (pbk.) | ISBN 9781508156635 (library bound) | ISBN 9781508156529 (6 pack)
Subjects: LCSH: Mongooses–Juvenile literature. | Cobras–Juvenile literature.
Classification: LCC QL737.C235 M47 2018 | DDC 599.74'2–dc23

Manufactured in the United States of America

CPSIA Compliance Information: Batch Batch #BS17PK: For Further Information contact Rosen Publishing, New York, New York at 1-800-237-9932

CONTENTS

LIFE IN SOUTHERN INDIA

Two deadly predators wander the forests of India. The king cobra slides across the ground, **slithers** up trees, and swims through streams, flicking its tongue to pick up the scent of other animals. Nearby, an Indian gray mongoose hides in the shadows, waiting for the right moment to dart out.

Mongooses enjoy eating king cobras, but one wrong move and the mongoose could end up on the cobra's menu instead! When the Indian gray mongoose is pitted against the king cobra, the hunter could very well become the hunted.

INDIA

INDIAN GRAY
MONGOOSE
AND COBRA
HABITAT

King cobras and Indian gray
mongooses can be found in India
and other parts of Asia.

MONGOOSE BASICS

There are more than 30 **species** of mongooses in the world. This book is about the Indian gray mongoose. Indian gray mongooses are small creatures weighing only about 2 to 4 pounds (0.9 to 1.8 kg). Their bodies measure 15 to 19 inches (38.1 to 48.3 cm) long, but their bushy tail is another 13 to 16 inches (33 to 40.6 cm) long.

As their name notes, Indian gray mongooses are usually gray or light brown. They have long, pointed noses, small, rounded ears, and short legs.

WILDLIFE WISDOM

"Rikki-Tikki-Tavi" is a story by Rudyard Kipling about a brave mongoose who takes on two cobras to **protect** a human family. First published in 1893, it's still the most popular story to be written about a mongoose. "Rikki-Tikki-Tavi" was included in Kipling's *The Jungle Book*.

INDIAN GRAY MONGOOSE

The many mongoose species are different sizes and colors.

BANDED MONGOOSE

DWARF MONGOOSE

A MONGOOSE'S LIFE

Indian gray mongooses like to be on their own most of the time, only coming together when it's time to **mate**. Female mongooses give birth to two or three litters each year. Each litter is made up of two to four pups who stay with their mother for the first six months of their lives.

Mongoose pups are ready to leave their mother when they're able to hunt. Indian gray mongooses are not picky eaters. They feed on scorpions, lizards, rats, snakes, and **carrion**.

Mongooses may make their homes in hollow parts of trees, underground, or in spaces between rocks.

MONGOOSE STRENGTHS

Although small, mongooses are strong hunters. Their sharp teeth and claws can tear **prey** to pieces. Indian gray mongooses are very fast, which helps when they're hunting and fighting. They're smart creatures and seem to plan their attacks. Some species of mongooses have even been known to use simple tools. For example, they'll break hard objects by hitting them on rocks.

Mongooses even have a secret strength—they can resist the venom, or poison, produced by many snakes and scorpions.

Mongooses live an average of seven years in the wild.

THE KING COBRA

There are about 270 species of cobras. This book focuses on king cobras. King cobras can be up to 18 feet (5.5 m) long. That's more than three times the height of an average person! King cobras are the longest venomous snakes in the world. King cobras may weigh up to 20 pounds (9 kg).

The most striking thing about king cobras is their hood. When they feel threatened, king cobras will lift the top part of their body and **expand** the ribs and muscles on their neck to form a hood.

A king cobra's hood can make it look bigger and more frightening to a predator. Cobras can lift a third of their body off the ground.

13

COBRA HATCHLINGS

A group of king cobras is called a quiver. King cobras prefer to be on their own, coming together only to mate. They are the only snakes known to build nests. Females push together pieces of grass and leaves to build a nest in which they'll lay their eggs.

WILDLIFE WISDOM

King cobras don't have ears on the outer parts of their bodies. Because of this, they don't have a very good sense of hearing. Instead, they sense vibrations, or movements, in the ground.

King cobras may live for 20 years in the wild. They reach adulthood when they're about four years old.

King cobras lay clutches, or groups, of 20 to 50 eggs. They cover the eggs with leaves and lay on top of them to keep them warm. When the eggs are ready to hatch, the mother king cobra leaves them.

THE COBRA'S BITE

King cobras eat lizards, rats, and other snakes. Snakes smell with their tongues. They pick up scents through **particles** in the air. Like all snakes, king cobras swallow their prey whole.

WILDLIFE WISDOM

For the most part, king cobras are shy and avoid humans. When they feel threatened, however, they can be very forceful. A king cobra's venom can kill a person in just 30 minutes. Cobra bites can be treated with drugs called antivenin, but 60 percent of untreated bites result in death.

One bite from a king cobra can have enough venom to kill 20 people! King cobras have special **glands** behind their eyes where venom is made. When they bite, they use two sharp teeth to **inject** the venom into their prey's body. The venom causes pain, **paralysis**, and finally death.

A king cobra's venom is so strong a cobra can kill an adult Asian elephant with just one bite.

17

FACE-OFF!

King cobras may be one of the world's deadliest animals, but they're one of the Indian gray mongoose's favorite foods! What happens when a mongoose takes on a cobra?

Few predators other than mongooses can kill a king cobra.

Sensing danger, the cobra rises up, expands its hood, and lets out a bone-chilling hiss. The mongoose bares its teeth, waiting for the right moment to attack. The mongoose is lightning-fast! It darts at the cobra and sinks its teeth into its neck. The mongoose is **immune** to small amounts of the cobra's venom, but too many bites can kill the mongoose.

KEEPING THE BALANCE

Indian gray mongooses have special **adaptations** that prepare them to take on king cobras. Mongooses have thick fur coats, which help guard against bites. King cobra venom causes paralysis. Unlike other animals, mongooses have specially adapted to block this venom and can fight cobras without becoming paralyzed.

Both species benefit from this hunter-and-hunted connection. King cobras are an important source of food for mongooses. King cobras benefit from being hunted by mongooses because if they weren't, their populations could grow to unhealthy numbers.

Which animal do you think is more scary—the mongoose or the cobra?

TEAM MONGOOSE VS. TEAM COBRA

Although they're small, Indian gray mongooses shouldn't be taken lightly. Their ability to move quickly and easily and their immunity to venom make them more than a match for a king cobra. In fact, a king cobra's only hope for survival when it's attacked by a mongoose is to flee or keep biting it.

These natural enemies are very evenly matched when it comes to the battle for survival. Which creature would you root for? Would you choose the king cobra with its venomous bite? Or would you choose the fast and fierce mongoose?

GLOSSARY

adaptation: A change in a living thing that helps it live better in a certain environment.

carrion: A dead, rotting animal.

expand: To become bigger.

gland: A body part that produces something that helps with a bodily function.

immune: Safe from something, often a sickness.

inject: To force something into a body using a needle or sharp teeth.

mate: One of two animals that come together to make babies or to come together to make babies.

paralysis: Loss of feeling and movement in a part of the body.

particles: Small pieces of matter.

prey: An animal that is hunted by another animal for food.

protect: To keep safe.

slither: To move smoothly over a surface with a side-to-side motion.

species: A group of plants or animals that are all the same kind.

INDEX

WEBSITES

Due to the changing nature of Internet links, PowerKids Press has developed an online list of websites related to the subject of this book. This site is updated regularly. Please use this link to access the list: www.powerkidslinks.com/handh/cobra